ROCKFORD PUBLIC LIBRARY

3 1112 018847448

W9-BII-228

J B K27 11
Garrett, Leslie
Helen Keller

WITHDRAWN

052113

ROCKFORD PUBLIC LIBRARY

Rockford, Illinois

www.rockfordpubliclibrary.org

815-965-9511

DK READERS

Level 3

Level 4

A Note to Parents

DK READERS is a compelling program for beginning readers, designed in conjunction with leading literacy experts, including Dr. Linda Gambrell, Distinguished Professor of Education at Clemson University. Dr. Gambrell has served as President of the National Reading Conference, the College Reading Association, and the International Reading Association.

Beautiful illustrations and superb full-color photographs combine with engaging, easy-to-read stories to offer a fresh approach to each subject in the series. Each DK READER is guaranteed to capture a child's interest while developing his or her reading skills, general knowledge, and love of reading.

The five levels of DK READERS are aimed at different reading abilities, enabling you to choose the books that are exactly right for your child:

Pre-level 1: Learning to read
Level 1: Beginning to read
Level 2: Beginning to read alone
Level 3: Reading alone
Level 4: Proficient readers

The "normal" age at which a child begins to read can be anywhere from three to eight years old. Adult participation through the lower levels is very helpful for providing encouragement, discussing storylines, and sounding out unfamiliar words.

No matter which level you select, you can be sure that you are helping your child learn to read, then read to learn!

LONDON, NEW YORK, MUNICH,
MELBOURNE, AND DELHI

DK LONDON
Series Editor Deborah Lock
Art Director Martin Wilson
US Editor Shannon Beatty
Production Editor Francesca Wardell
Jacket Designer Martin Wilson
Illustrator Stuart@kja-artists.com

DK DELHI
Senior Editor Priyanka Nath
Senior Art Editor Rajnish Kashyap
Assistant Editor Deeksha Saikia
Assistant Designer Dhirendra Singh, Tanvi Sahu
DTP Designer Anita Yadav
Picture Researcher Sumedha Chopra
Managing Editor Alka Thakur Hazarika
Managing Art Editor Romi Chakraborty

Reading Consultant
Linda B. Gambrell, Ph.D.
Subject Consultant
Helen Selsdon, Archivist,
American Foundation for the Blind

First American Edition, 2013
Published in the United States by DK Publishing
375 Hudson Street, New York, New York 10014

13 14 15 16 17 10 9 8 7 6 5 4 3 2 1
001—187466—June/2013

Copyright © 2013 Dorling Kindersley Limited
All rights reserved.
Without limiting the rights under copyright reserved above, no part of this publication
may be reproduced, stored in or introduced into a retrieval system, or transmitted, in any
form, or by any means (electronic, mechanical, photocopying, recording, or otherwise),
without the prior written permission of the copyright owner.
Published in Great Britain by Dorling Kindersley Limited.

A catalog record for this book is available
from the Library of Congress.
ISBN: 978-1-46540-946-1 (Paperback)
ISBN: 978-1-46540-947-8 (Hardcover)

DK books are available at special discounts when purchased in bulk
for sales promotions, premiums, fund-raising, or educational use.
For details, contact:
DK Publishing Special Markets
375 Hudson Street, New York, New York 10014
SpecialSales@dk.com

Color reproduction by Colourscan, Singapore
Printed and bound in China by L Rex Printing Co., Ltd.

The publisher would like to thank the following for their kind
permission to reproduce their photographs:

(Key: a-above; b-below/bottom; c-center; f-far; l-left; r-right; t-top)

1 Corbis: (br). 3 Perkins School for the Blind: (cb). 5 Getty Images: Southern
Stock / Photodisc (br). 6 Alamy Images: Andre Jenny (tl). 9 Perkins School for
the Blind: (br). 11 Perkins School for the Blind: (br). 16 Helen Keller Birth
Place: (tl). 17 Perkins School for the Blind: (b). 24 Perkins School for the
Blind: (tl, br). 26 Perkins School for the Blind: (t). 27 Perkins School for the
Blind: (br). 28-29 Perkins School for the Blind: (bc). 30 Getty Images: Time &
Life Pictures (tl). 31 Dorling Kindersley: The Science Museum, London (br).
Getty Images: Dr. Gilbert H. Grosvenor / National Geographic. 34 Perkins
School for the Blind. 35 Alamy Images: eye35 (br). 37 Corbis: Bettmann (br).
38 TopFoto.co.uk: Sarah Fabian-Baddiel / HIP (tl). 39 Corbis: Hulton-Deutsch
Collection (t). Helen Keller Birth Place: (br). 40 Perkins School for the Blind: (bl).
41 Corbis: John Springer Collection (br). Perkins School for the Blind: (tl).
42 Perkins School for the Blind: (b). 43 Perkins School for the Blind: (bl).
44 Corbis: Bettmann. 45 Alamy Images: Eye-Stock. 46 Corbis: Bettmann (tr).
Perkins School for the Blind: (bl). 47 Corbis: Bettmann (br)

Jacket images: Front: Corbis: Library of Congress - digital ve / Science Faction

All other images © Dorling Kindersley
For further information see: www.dkimages.com

Discover more at
www.dk.com

Contents

DK READERS

Helen Keller

Written by Leslie Garrett

DK Publishing

ROCKFORD PUBLIC LIBRARY

A remarkable lady

Helen Keller ran her fingers across the pages of her Braille book, taking in every word.

Finishing the last page, she closed her book and placed it on the table beside her bed. At 87 years old, although she was still fairly active, she was growing tired. Blind and deaf since the age of 19 months, Helen knew she was lucky to be able to read and write. She leaned back on her pillow and closed her eyes, thinking back on her remarkable life.

Braille
Braille is a method blind people use to read. Created by Louis Braille, the alphabet, numbers, punctuation, and speech sounds are represented by different combinations of six raised dots arranged in a grid.

Fever and frustration

Ivy Green, the house in which Helen was born

Helen was born in Tuscumbia, Alabama, on June 27, 1880. She was born able to see and hear. When she was 19 months old, she developed a very high fever. Doctors didn't think she would survive, but finally the fever broke. Over the next few days, however, Helen's parents noticed their daughter didn't turn away from bright light. She didn't respond to the dinner bell.

The Kellers traveled from doctor to doctor, sure that someone could help their daughter.

But the answer was always
the same. Helen was destined to
live her life in darkness and silence.

The little girl was resourceful and clever though. Desperate to communicate, she used signs to show people what she was unable to say. Before long Helen had more than 60 signs. But she was so often frustrated with no way to ask questions.

She threw angry fits, throwing things and breaking them.

Helen's parents indulged her and gave in to her tantrums. However, when her baby sister was born and Helen tipped her out of the cradle in anger, her parents decided something must be done. Her father wrote to the Perkins Institution for blind children to request a teacher.

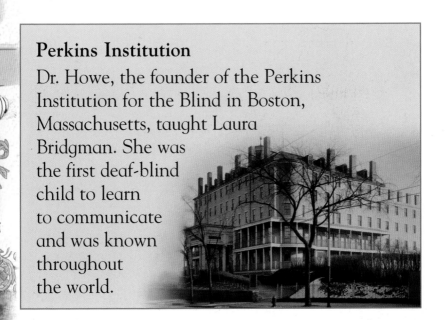

Perkins Institution
Dr. Howe, the founder of the Perkins Institution for the Blind in Boston, Massachusetts, taught Laura Bridgman. She was the first deaf-blind child to learn to communicate and was known throughout the world.

Helen knew something was
up that lovely March day in 1887.
All day, everyone had been rushing
around her. She was right. Annie
Sullivan from the Perkins Institution
had accepted the job
as Helen's teacher.

Annie was surprised when she first met Helen. Helen rushed toward Annie, holding out her arms. She believed Annie to be her mother. But when Annie hugged her, she pulled away like a strong, wild young colt. Who was this stranger?

That night, Annie lay in her bed tossing and turning, wondering how she was ever going to teach this wild child anything.

Annie Sullivan
Annie Sullivan had been a student at Perkins after losing her sight as a child. Operations eventually restored her vision, but she never saw very well and often wore dark glasses.

Helen's curiosity drew her back to the stranger. In Annie's room, Helen plunged her hands into the stranger's suitcase. Annie watched while Helen searched for something familiar. She pulled out a doll and hugged it close.

Annie picked up Helen's hand. D-O-L-L she spelled with her finger in Helen's palm. Helen didn't understand what Annie was trying to do.

Annie knew that if she could
teach Helen to communicate,
she'd become a different child—
a happier child.

Taming the wild child

Annie was shocked when she first sat down to eat with the Keller family. They allowed Helen to wander around the table, taking food from everyone's plate and stuffing it in her mouth. Helen threw so many temper tantrums that the family just let her do what she wanted, a practice Annie strongly disagreed with. One tantrum was so bad, Helen knocked out one of Annie's teeth. Finally, Annie told Helen's mother that she wanted to take Helen away with her. Only when Helen relied on Annie alone could love and trust be established.

The house where Annie took Helen

Annie and Helen moved to a cottage on the Kellers' property. Helen's father checked on his daughter daily, but Helen never knew he was watching. Slowly, as the spring days passed, Helen settled down. She fought less hard and less often. Annie continued to teach Helen every day, trying to reach the little girl in her dark, silent world.

She was often spelling the words of things into the palm of Helen's hand.

Even though Helen often spelled the letters back, to her it was just a game. She didn't understand that the letters made words and described things.

T-E-A-C-H-E-R

Helen loved playing in the cool ground around the water pump. One beautiful day, a month after Annie's arrival, Annie put Helen's hands under the cool water. W-A-T-E-R, she spelled into Helen's palm. Helen's face seemed to brighten. Quickly, Annie did it again. W-A-T-E-R. W-A-T-E-R. In an instant, Helen understood. Everything had a name.

The little girl was excited. She rushed around touching everything so Annie could tell her what it was. D-I-R-T, spelled Annie. Then, H-E-L-E-N. Finally, T-E-A-C-H-E-R. Before the day was through, Helen had learned to make 30 word shapes.

Helen was ready for the next step. Annie pulled out a big card with the 26 letters of the alphabet written in raised lettering. This was how the blind learned to read. She placed Helen's hand on the letter A. Then she spelled the letter into Helen's palm. She did the same for B. Then C. Suddenly Helen understood. By the end of the day, Helen had learned all the letters of the alphabet.

Annie wrote in a letter to a friend: "Something within me tells me that I shall succeed beyond my dreams."

Annie was determined that
Helen would be able to take part in
the world around her. She showed
Helen what happened when a seed
was planted in the ground. Helen
learned to tell trees apart by touch.
She felt an egg hatch in her hand.
Annie also wanted Helen to know
about things that happened far away
and long ago and she wanted Helen
to understand ideas and thoughts.

One day, while Helen puzzled over
a very hard question, Annie tapped
Helen's forehead. T-H-I-N-K, she
spelled. Helen immediately
understood. That was what she
was doing—she was thinking.

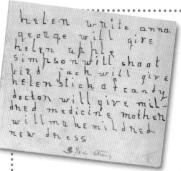

One of Helen's early writing attempts

Helen was also writing. She learned to write in the summer of 1887. Annie gave her a grooved writing board that was placed over a sheet of paper. Helen wrote the letters between the grooves, guiding the pencil with her right hand and checking the shape and size of the letters with the forefinger of her left hand. Annie insisted that Helen keep a journal, which she did for most of her life.

Skills for life
Annie taught Helen to dress nicely, walk upright, and behave graciously. She also encouraged Helen to always have a smile on her face.

Into the outside world

In the spring of 1888, Annie and Helen received an invitation from the Perkins Institution to come for a visit. Helen loved it. She could play with other girls and boys, but most of all she loved the books. Helen learned to read hundreds of books in raised print and Braille. However, when Helen returned home, she was eager to learn more.

Annie often became tired spelling hour after hour into Helen's hand. Helen also grew frustrated. The thoughts in her head came so rapidly that people could barely understand her quick signing. Then Helen had an idea. She would learn how to speak.

Helen (sitting) fingerspelling into the hand of her friend, Edith Thomas.

At first, Annie discouraged Helen from trying to learn to speak. After all, the little girl had no way to watch people's mouths or hear their words. Helen persisted and finally won her over. Annie took Helen back to Boston and hired a teacher, Sarah Fuller, who taught blind children to talk.

Helen practiced until her mouth felt dry and swollen. One day she opened her mouth and, in a growly voice—part shout, part whisper—said, "It is warm."

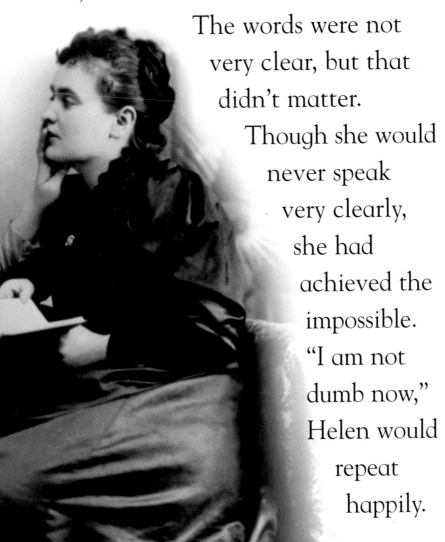

The words were not very clear, but that didn't matter.

Though she would never speak very clearly, she had achieved the impossible. "I am not dumb now," Helen would repeat happily.

President Grover Cleveland

As Helen achieved more and more, word about this incredible child began to spread. Newspapers ran stories about her. Famous people contacted her. She was even invited to meet Grover Cleveland, the president of the United States. She became friends with his wife.

With so many invitations from people for Helen to visit, Annie usually chose to meet those who could help Helen the most. Helen spent time with a friend of the family, Alexander Graham Bell. He was not only the inventor of the telephone but also a teacher of deaf people.

Helen feels Annie's lips while using sign language to communicate with Alexander Graham Bell.

Bell's telephone inventions

On March 10, 1876, Alexander Graham Bell and his assistant Thomas Watson were the first to discover how to transmit the human voice over long distances.

College dreams

Despite all the interest, Helen spent most of her days like other children. She loved to ride her horse, walk her dogs, take bike rides, and swim. She also came up with her next goal.

"Some day I shall go to college," Helen told her friends and Annie, "but I shall go to Harvard!"

Though Annie thought the dream impossible, she had learned not to doubt her young student. So, she answered simply, "Not Harvard, Helen. Harvard is for boys."

For four years, Helen spent much time in Boston studying. She was determined to get into Radcliffe, a highly respected women's college. When the president of the college said she couldn't attend because she wouldn't be able to keep up with the other girls, Helen was furious. She replied in a letter, "You must let me try."

She won. In the fall of 1900, Helen Keller enrolled at Radcliffe College in Cambridge, Massachusetts.

College for girls
Opened in 1879, Radcliffe College was created to offer an education to women who were unable to go to boys-only Harvard University.

College was not easy for Helen. Annie attended classes with her, spelling into Helen's hands what the professor was saying.

But, Annie could not spell fast enough and parts of the lesson were missed. No notes were taken so Helen relied completely on her incredible memory for her essays and tests.

In 1904, Helen graduated *cum laude*—with honors. She was the best-educated blind-deaf person in the world.

The cover of a copy of the Ladies Home Journal

While at college, the *Ladies Home Journal* asked Helen to write a story about her life. With the help of John Macy, an editor, Helen put together a series of articles that eventually became *The Story of My Life.* In 1903, this became Helen's first of 14 books to be published.

Helen put the money toward buying a house near Boston with Annie. After graduating, Helen decided she'd continue to support herself and Annie with her writing.

Out of the Dark

In 1913, Helen wrote *Out of the Dark*. It was about solving the world's problems and stated that women should be able to vote and that the United States should stay out of any wars. The book was a flop.

Telling the world

When writing didn't make enough money, Helen decided she would travel and give speeches about the barriers facing blind and deaf people. She was a popular speaker, and she and Annie traveled widely.

When an idea for a movie about her life fell through, Helen developed

a vaudeville act for herself and Annie. The live show featured Annie telling the story of Helen's life.

Poster of Deliverance, *a play that featured Helen*

Annie and Helen's publicity shot taken around 1920

Helen then showed the audience that she could "feel" them clapping. She would answer their questions that Annie spelled into her palm. Helen loved the shows and felt she was helping people. Annie hated them.

Showtime

Vaudeville was variety stage shows that included short acts such as singing, dancing, juggling, and comedy. They were the most popular form of entertainment in America between 1875 and 1932.

Eventually, the popularity of the shows faded. Annie was exhausted from performing so the women stopped. Helen took a job with the American Foundation for the Blind, lobbying for education and equal opportunities for blind people.

She gave speeches, telling others all that blind people can do and achieve. In her first three years, she spoke to 250,000 people in 123 American cities. She loved the work.

In 1931, Helen and Annie were both awarded honorary college degrees from Temple University in Philadelphia, Pennsylvania. At the ceremony, Annie refused to accept her degree. She believed that her success with Helen was due to Helen's  cleverness, not her teaching. However, the crowd rose to its feet and at last Annie accepted the honor.

On October 20, 1936, Helen's beloved teacher died at the age of 70. Helen could not bear to be at home without Annie, so she began traveling again with her secretary Polly Thomson. One of the 39 countries she visited was Japan. The government held parties and gave her presents. It boosted Helen and Polly and gave them a reason to continue raising awareness about people with vision loss.

When Helen returned to the United States, she was shocked and saddened when Japan bombed Pearl Harbor, bringing the country into World War II.

Movie success
In 1959, a play about Annie and Helen called *The Miracle Worker* was performed in New York City. It later became an award-winning movie.

Helen spent the war years visiting wounded soldiers, many of whom were now blind. She found the work most rewarding, giving these men back a sense of hope for the future. She remained determined to prove to the world that not only could she do anything, other disabled people could

also. She continued giving speeches for the American Foundation for the Blind.

She lived in Connecticut, at her home, Arcan Ridge, named after a favorite place in Scotland.

She also continued to write, including publishing a book about Annie. Helen Keller died in her sleep on June 1, 1968, shortly before her 88th birthday.

Glossary

American Foundation for the Blind
This organization was founded in 1921 to provide people who are blind or have vision loss with information and resources.

Article
A non-fiction piece of writing for a newspaper or magazine.

Blind
Unable to see.

Braille
A written language for the blind, using patterns of raised dots felt with the fingertips.

College
A place of higher education where students go to study courses to gain degrees and diplomas.

Cum laude
Latin words meaning "with honors."

Deaf
Unable to hear.

Degree
An educational title given by a college or university to a student when he or she has completed a course.

Enrolled
To enter a person's name on to a list for a college or a class.

Fever
A very high body temperature caused by a disease or virus.

Graduation
A ceremony for students when they celebrate receiving their degrees or diplomas.

Honorary college degree
A degree given by a college to a person who deserves to be recognized for something they have achieved.

Honors
A special title for recognizing high achievement.

Lobbying
Trying to persuade government officials to support a cause.

Perkins Institution for the Blind
This school was founded in 1832 to provide education for children and adults who are blind, deaf-blind, or have vision loss.

Professor
A high-ranking teacher in a college or university.

Signing
A way of communicating a word or thought with a hand gesture.

Vaudeville
A stage show that featured a number of people performing in different ways, such as comedians, singers, dancers, and acrobats. This type of entertainment was popular in the US in the early 20th century.

World War II
A war between 1939 and 1945 that involved many of the countries around the world.

Index